The Vacation Countdown is ON
A Guidebook for Planning the Perfect Trip

Kulana Media Productions LLC

CONTENTS

ABOUT THIS BOOK

Welcome to **"The Vacation Countdown Is On: A Guidebook for Planning the Perfect Trip"**!

At Vacation Countdown App[1], we've been helping people plan and get excited about their upcoming vacations since 2014, when we first published our free app. We've seen millions of app users looking forward to their upcoming trips with joy and know firsthand the importance of building excitement for a vacation. But we also recognize that excitement is just one piece of the puzzle.

Our website, which we launched in 2020, is a helpful addition to our app and a valuable resource for vacation planning, featuring a wide range of helpful tips and ideas to get you started on your vacation planning journey. However, we wanted to take it a step further and provide a comprehensive guidebook that covers every aspect of vacation planning. That's why we've created this guidebook - to provide step-by-step guidance on every aspect of vacation planning. From choosing the right destination and setting a budget to making travel arrangements and packing efficiently, we cover everything you need to know to plan a stress-free vacation. We've also included a collection of travel poems to inspire your wanderlust and make the planning process even more enjoyable.

So, whether you're a seasoned traveler or planning your first vacation, we hope this book will help you make the most of your time off and create unforgettable memories.

---

[1] www.vacationcountdownapp.com

1. INTRODUCTION TO VACATION PLANNING

Vacation planning is about taking control of your time off and creating a trip that meets your needs and desires. By putting in the time and effort to plan ahead, you can save money, choose the best destination for your needs, and ensure you have an unforgettable vacation.

In this chapter, we'll cover the importance of taking time off and explore how to choose the right destination for your trip. We'll discuss a budget, make travel arrangements, create an itinerary, and pack efficiently. By the end of this chapter, you'll be well on your way to planning your dream vacation.

Let's get started!

The Importance of Taking Time Off

Vacation is an essential component of maintaining a healthy work-life balance. It gives us the opportunity to step away from our daily routine, relax, and recharge. Research has consistently shown that taking time off has numerous benefits, including improved mental health, increased productivity, and stronger relationships.

According to a study by the American Psychological Association (APA), taking a vacation can reduce the risk of developing burnout and decrease stress levels. In fact, the study found that people who take vacations regularly report higher levels of satisfaction with their job and life overall. Taking time off can also improve physical health, as it allows us to relax and recharge, which can lower our risk of developing certain chronic conditions.

But despite these benefits, many people struggle to take time off. According to a study by Project: Time Off, 55% of Americans did not use all of their vacation days in 2019. This may be due to overwhelming work demands or a sense of responsibility towards their responsibilities. But failing to take time off can have negative consequences as well. Burnout, stress, and a lack of work-life balance can lead to decreased productivity, poor mental and physical health, and strained relationships.

So how do you determine how much vacation time you need? Finding the right balance is crucial. Consider your personal goals, work demands, and overall health and well-being. It's also a good idea to check with your employer about available vacation time and how it can be used.

In conclusion, taking time off is essential for your physical and mental health, relationships, and productivity. Don't be afraid to take the time you need to recharge and come back to work feeling refreshed and energized.

The Benefits of Planning a Vacation in Advance

Planning a vacation can have numerous benefits that can enhance your overall travel experience. Some of the main advantages include the following:

Reduced stress

When you have a clear plan, you can stay organized and on top of things, making the vacation planning process much less overwhelming. This can also give you peace of mind, knowing that everything is taken care of, and you can simply focus on enjoying your time off.

Increased enjoyment

By scheduling activities and making reservations ahead of time, you can ensure that you are making the most of your vacation and not wasting valuable time trying to figure out what to do. This can also make you more spontaneous and flexible, as you won't have to worry about finding last-minute options or dealing with crowds and long lines.

Better prices and availability

Planning early often leads to better prices on flights, accommodations, and activities. It can also increase your chances of securing your desired options, as popular choices can fill up quickly.

More time to save and prepare

Planning a vacation in advance can give you more time to save money and prepare for your trip. This can include researching your destination, making a packing list, and obtaining any necessary travel documents or visas.

Improved travel experience

A well-planned vacation can lead to a more enjoyable and memorable experience overall. By planning your trip carefully, you can ensure that you are fully prepared and can fully relax and enjoy your time off.

Tips For Planning a Smooth Vacation

Planning a vacation can be overwhelming, but there are several steps you can take to make the process as smooth as possible.

Here are a few tips to consider:

1. **Set a budget and stick to it**
Determine how much you can afford to spend on your vacation, and make sure you stick to it. This will help you make informed decisions and avoid overspending. Remember to factor in the cost of flights, accommodations, activities, meals, and any other expenses you may incur.

2. **Make a list of the things you want to do and see**
Determine your must-see and must-do list and prioritize accordingly. This will help you make the most of your time and ensure you take advantage of all must-see attractions. Consider the interests and preferences of all travelers, the length of your vacation, and the amount of time you have available for activities.

3. **Research your destination**
Look for the best flights and accommodations and learn about local attractions and activities. This will help you

create a well-rounded vacation plan that includes a mix of relaxation and adventure. Consider the weather, cultural customs, and any special events or festivals that may be happening during your trip.

4. Make reservations and bookings
This includes flights, accommodations, and any activities or tours you want to do. You can often get better deals and secure your spot in popular activities by booking in advance. Make sure to read reviews and compare prices to find the best options for your budget and preferences.

5. Create a packing list
Make a list of everything you need to bring, and pack as efficiently as possible. This will help you avoid overpacking and ensure you have everything you need for your dream vacation. Remember to include essentials like identification, travel documents, medications, and any necessary travel adaptors or chargers.

By following these tips, you can confidently plan a stress-free and enjoyable vacation. While it may take some time and effort upfront, the benefits of having a well-planned vacation can far outweigh the initial planning process. Planning ahead can reduce stress, increase enjoyment, secure better prices and availability, provide more time to save and prepare, and improve your overall travel experience. In addition to these practical benefits, planning can also have psychological benefits.

According to studies, the anticipation and planning of a vacation can be just as rewarding as the vacation itself. The planning process gives us control and can provide a sense of accomplishment and happiness. So, take the time to plan your dream vacation carefully, and you'll be on your way to a relaxing and enjoyable trip that will bring you joy before and during your vacation.

Choosing the Right Destination

When choosing a vacation destination, there are several important factors to consider finding the location that best suits your needs and preferences. These factors include:

Climate

One crucial factor to consider is the weather and vacation experience you want. Do you want to relax on a sunny beach like Bali or the Caribbean? Or would you prefer to hit the slopes in a ski destination like Whistler or Aspen? Or do you want to explore a bustling city like Paris or New York? Think about the weather and environment you enjoy and look for destinations that offer those conditions.

Culture

Are you interested in immersing yourself in a new culture or prefer to stick to a more familiar destination? Consider the cultural activities that interest you and look for destinations that offer those experiences. For example, if you love trying new foods, consider a destination with a vibrant food scene, like Vietnam or Italy. Or, if you're interested in history and art, destinations like Egypt or Spain might be a good fit.

Activities and attractions

What do you want to do on your vacation? Do you want to spend your days exploring museums, trying new foods, or relaxing on the beach? Consider the activities and attractions available at your potential destination and how they align with your vacation goals. Research online or reach out to local tourism boards or travel agencies for recommendations on the best things to do and see.

Budget

Determine how much you can afford to spend on your vacation and look for destinations that fit within your budget. Remember that some destinations may have additional fees or taxes that may not be included in the initial price, so be sure to factor those in when making your decision. To find the best deals, consider signing up for alerts or newsletters from travel companies, using price comparison websites, and being flexible with travel dates.

Other factors

Other factors to consider when choosing a destination include the distance and mode of transportation, accessibility for travelers with disabilities, and any language barriers that may be present. By considering these factors and researching, you can find the perfect destination for your dream vacation. So, take the time to consider your options and make an informed decision carefully, and you'll be well on your way to a relaxing and enjoyable trip.

Determining the Type of Vacation That Best Suits Your Needs

When planning the perfect vacation, it's important to determine the type of vacation that best suits your needs and preferences. To do this, you should consider various factors, including your personal preferences, logistical considerations, and destination-specific factors. Personal preferences include your vacation goals, who you are traveling with, your budget, your interests and hobbies, and your preferred climate and geography. Logistical considerations include your travel style, trip length, physical abilities, and the type of accommodation you choose. Destination-specific factors include your travel preferences, travel time required to reach your destination, visa requirements, transportation options, safety, language, cultural differences, and accessibility. Considering these factors, you can find the perfect vacation to suit your needs and make your dream trip a reality.

PERSONAL PREFERENCES

- **Your vacation goals:** Do you want to relax and unwind, have an adventure, or immerse yourself in culture? This can help narrow down your options and ensure that you choose a vacation that aligns with your priorities.

- **Travel companions:** Are you traveling solo, with a partner, or with friends or family? This can impact the type of vacation most suitable for you, as specific destinations and activities may be more suitable for certain groups.

- **Your budget:** Determine how much time and money you have to spend on your vacation and look for destinations and activities that align with your budget.

- **Your interests and hobbies:** Consider what activities and attractions you enjoy and look for destinations that offer those experiences. This can help ensure that you have an enjoyable and memorable trip.

- **Your preferred climate and geography:** Do you want to relax on a sunny beach, hit the slopes, or explore a bustling city? Choosing a destination that aligns with your preferred climate and geography can help ensure that you have a comfortable and enjoyable trip.

- **Type of accommodation:** Think about the type of accommodation you prefer – do you want a hotel, a vacation rental, or something else? Different types of accommodations offer various amenities and experiences, so consider your preferences when choosing your vacation destination.

- **Food and dining preferences:** Consider your food and dining preferences when choosing your vacation destination. Do you want to try new and exotic foods, or do you prefer familiar, comfortable options? Look for destinations that offer the type of food and dining experiences that align with your preferences.

LOGISTICAL CONSIDERATIONS

- **Travel Style:** Think about your preferred travel style – do you enjoy luxury and comfort, or are you more of a budget-conscious traveler? Different types of vacations cater to different travel styles, so be sure to consider your preferences when choosing your destination.

- **Length of trip:** How much time do you have available for your vacation? If you only have a few days, choose a destination closer to home or easier to get to. On the other hand, if you have more time available, consider a more extended, more immersive vacation.

- **Physical abilities:** If you have any physical limitations or disabilities, it's essential to consider how those might impact your vacation. For example, if you have mobility issues, you may want to choose a destination that is more accessible or has plenty of options for accessible activities.

DESTINATION-SPECIFIC FACTORS

- **Travel preferences:** Consider your preferences for transportation, accommodation, and other travel-related factors. Do you prefer flying or taking the train, staying in a hotel or a vacation rental, or exploring on your own or with a guided tour? Thinking about these preferences can help you find the perfect vacation for you.

- **Travel time:** How much time do you have available for your vacation? Are you able to take a more extended trip, or are you limited to a shorter, more focused trip? This can help narrow down your destination options and guide your decision on the type of vacation you choose.

- **Visa requirements:** Depending on your destination, you may need a visa to enter the country. Research the visa requirements for your desired destination and ensure you have the necessary documents and information to apply for a visa.

- **Transportation options:** Consider the transportation options available at your desired destination. Are there reliable and convenient ways to get around, such as public transportation or rental cars? Will you need to book transportation in advance, or can you easily arrange it on arrival?

- **Safety:** Research the safety of your desired destination and consider any potential risks or concerns. Some destinations may have higher crime rates or health risks, so it's important to be aware of these factors and take appropriate precautions.

- **Language and cultural differences:** If you are traveling to a destination with a different language or culture, consider the language barriers and cultural differences you may encounter. Consider taking language classes or hiring a guide to help navigate these differences and ensure a smoother, more enjoyable trip.

By considering these factors, you can determine the type of vacation that best suits your needs and make the most of your time away.

2. SETTING A BUDGET

Planning a vacation can be an enjoyable process filled with excitement and anticipation. However, it's imperative to consider budgeting when planning your vacation. For that reason, having a comprehensive budget plan is essential for helping you make informed decisions on destinations, accommodations, and activities.

This chapter covers the steps to creating a budget for your vacation: from setting both a total budget and daily budget to tips for staying within the boundaries of your allotted spending. If you follow these steps by committing to your budget plan, you can have a financially viable and unforgettable vacation.

Consider Your Overall Financial Situation

When setting a budget for a vacation, it's important to consider your overall financial situation. This includes both your current financial goals and your overall financial stability.

One key aspect of your overall financial situation to consider is any long-term financial goals, such as saving for retirement or paying off debt. If you are saving for a long-term goal or trying to pay off debt, you may need to allocate a smaller budget for your vacation. This can help ensure that you keep your other financial goals and put yourself in a manageable financial position.

On the other hand, if you have a stable financial situation and no pressing financial commitments, you may have more flexibility in your vacation budget.

By considering your overall financial situation first, you can set a realistic and responsible total budget for your vacation. This will help you make informed decisions about your destination, accommodations, and activities and ensure that you don't overspend.

Determine Your Total Budget

Before you start planning your dream vacation, it's important to determine how much money you have available or are willing to spend. This will help you make informed decisions about your destination, accommodations, and activities and ensure that you don't overspend.

To determine your total budget, consider the following factors:

- **Your financial situation**: How much disposable income do you have for your vacation? Do you have any savings set aside specifically for your vacation?

- **Time constraints:** How much time do you have to take a vacation? This will help you determine how long your vacation can be and how much you need to budget for flights, accommodations, and activities.

- **Other commitments**: Do you have any other financial obligations you need to prioritize, such as paying off debt or saving for a future goal? If so, allocate a smaller budget for your vacation.

Setting a specific amount aside for your vacation budget is better than using credit cards or dipping into savings because it helps you stay within your budget and avoids overspending. Credit cards can be tempting to use and may lead to impulse purchases that take away from your budget.

Additionally, if you dip into savings, it could put stress on the rest of your finances. Setting a specific amount aside allows you to stay within your budget and ensure you don't overspend. This will help keep your vacation financially successful and enjoyable.

Consider Your Vacation Goals and Priorities

When setting a budget for your vacation, it's important to consider your goals and priorities. What do you want to get out of this vacation? What activities and experiences are must-haves, and what are nice-to-haves that you can cut if needed? Answering these questions will help you prioritize your spending and ensure that your budget aligns with your goals and priorities.

To determine your goals and priorities, it can be helpful to brainstorm a list of must-have activities, accommodations, and experiences that you want from this vacation. This list should include anything that is essential for the experience you are trying to achieve with your vacation. Once you have determined what is necessary, you can decide which activities and experiences are nice-to-haves that you could eliminate if needed.

For example, a list for an outdoor exploration vacation may

include the following must-haves: camping gear, transportation to and from the campsite, supplies for hiking/fishing/etc., and access to trails. The nice-to-haves may include additional equipment or luxuries, such as a hotel stay for one night.

Another example is a list for a beach vacation that may include the following must-haves: beach access, sunscreen, swimsuits, and hotel/lodging. The nice-to-haves may consist of snorkeling gear, additional beach activities, or a rental car.

By creating a list of must-haves and nice-to-haves, you can prioritize your spending to ensure that your budget covers the essentials while still allowing room for some fun extras. Informed spending decisions will help make sure that your vacation is both enjoyable and financially successful.

Set a Daily Budget

Once you have determined your total budget, it's time to set a daily budget. This will help you plan for day-to-day expenses and give you an idea of how much money you have available each day for meals, activities, and other purchases. To determine your daily budget, divide the total amount by the number of days of your trip.

For example, if your total budget for a five-day trip is $1,000, your daily budget would be $200. However, it's important to remember that some of this money will need to go towards transportation costs such as flights or train tickets. Make sure to factor those in when determining your daily budget.

It's also important to track your spending throughout the duration of your trip to help you stay on track and avoid overspending. You can do this manually with a notebook or smartphone or use an app for easy tracking.

Remember to set aside a contingency fund for any unexpected expenses that may arise during your trip. Unexpected costs can quickly add up, so this fund will ensure you stay within budget and maintain the financial success of your vacation.

By setting a daily budget and tracking your spending throughout the trip, you can be confident that you are staying within your means and using your money wisely.

Tips For Sticking to Your Budget

Sticking to a budget for a vacation can be challenging, but it is possible with proper planning and discipline.

Here are some tips to help you stick to your budget:

1. **Plan Ahead:** Planning is key to budgeting success. Research your destination, look up prices for different activities and accommodations, and get an idea of what you want to do before you arrive. This will help you set realistic expectations and a more accurate budget.

2. **Set a Limit:** Establish a spending limit for yourself before you leave - and stick to it. Decide in advance how much money you are willing to spend on things like meals, activities, souvenirs, etc.; once you reach your limit, don't spend any more.

3. **Take Advantage of Deals**: Search for discounts or deals that can help you save money. You can often find reduced prices on activities and accommodations if you look in the right places. Try using discount search engines or coupons to help you save money on your vacation expenses.

4. **Prioritize**: Prioritize what is important to you and focus your budget on those things first before taking off-budget luxuries. This will help you ensure that the most critical aspects of your trip are covered and that you don't have to sacrifice too much.

5. **Track Your Spending**: Tracking your spending is key to sticking to a budget. Use an app or keep a notebook with you so you can easily monitor how much money you spend throughout your trip.

6. **Make Smart Choices**: You don't have to spend a lot of money on vacation to have a good time. Make smart choices and look for inexpensive activities or meals that are still enjoyable.

These tips can help you stay on budget and make your vacation financially successful. With careful planning, discipline, and informed spending decisions, you can ensure that your vacation is both an enjoyable and cost-effective experience!

3. MAKING TRAVEL ARRANGEMENTS

Making travel arrangements is an integral part of planning any vacation, no matter the destination or mode of transportation. In this chapter of our Vacation Planning Guidebook, we will focus on tips for using flights as your primary mode of transportation, as flying is typically the quickest and most efficient way to get to a far-off destination.

We will cover topics such as booking flights and accommodations, the importance of reading reviews before booking, and a checklist of things to consider when choosing flights and accommodations.

Booking Flights

Booking a flight is not as intimidating as it may seem. With the help of online travel search engines, booking flights has become increasingly easier in recent years. You can find great deals on flights and compare prices for multiple airfare providers with just a few clicks.

You can also use a travel agent for booking flights and other travel arrangements. Travel agents often have access to great deals that aren't available online, plus they make the entire process of finding the best flight deal much simpler. A good travel agent will take into consideration your budget, destination, and preferences before recommending the best flight option for you.

When booking a flight, consider the following factors first:

- **Flight duration:** How long will your flight be? Do you want to fly non-stop or with layovers?

- **Airlines and partnerships**: Which airlines offer flights to your destination? If you are enrolled in any airline loyalty programs, which companies offer the best rewards?

- **Flight prices**: How much will your flight cost? Are there any discounts or sales available?

- **Flexibility and cancellation policies**: Are you able to cancel or reschedule the flight if needed? What are the penalties for doing so?

Understanding Different Types of Tickets

When booking a flight, you may encounter different ticket types. It is important to understand the differences between these tickets before making a purchase as certain restrictions apply to each type of ticket.

The three most common types of airline tickets are:

- Economy/Coach
- Business Class
- First Class

Each type of ticket offers different levels of service and amenities. Economy tickets are the most economical but offer fewer benefits than business or first-class tickets. Business class tickets often provide more legroom and larger seats, while first-class tickets typically offer luxury perks such as complimentary meals and drinks, priority boarding, access to exclusive lounges, etc.

The airline you choose is just as important as the type of ticket. When researching different airlines, keep in mind these factors:

- **Cost:** Compare prices between different airlines and consider the cost of taxes and fees.

- **Reviews:** Read customer reviews to ensure your chosen airline meets your needs.

- **Baggage Policies:** Research the airline's baggage policies, particularly if you are an international traveler.

- **In-Flight Services:** If you will be traveling with children or have special needs, consider the in-flight services offered by different airlines.

- **Flight Times:** Check the flight times to find the most convenient option for your trip. Different airlines might be flying to your destination but at different times. Choose the one that best suits your schedule.

- **Additional Fees:** Some airlines charge additional fees for meals, seat selection, extra baggage, etc. Be sure to inquire about any other fees that may apply.

- **Cancellation Policies:** Check the cancellation policies of different airlines and compare them to find the most flexible option.

Now that you understand how to book a flight let's move on

to selecting accommodations for your vacation.

Booking Accommodations

Once you've found the perfect flight, it's time to book your accommodations. There are various types of accommodations available, from hotels and resorts to hostels and Airbnb rentals.

Choosing the Right Location

Choosing the right location for your vacation accommodation can significantly enhance your relaxation and enjoyment throughout the trip. To make sure you pick the perfect spot, research different locations thoroughly to get a better sense of which one best fits your needs.

Consider factors such as proximity to local attractions and public transportation, price range, availability of restaurants and activities in the area, the safety of the environment, access to parking, and other amenities offered. Be sure to read up on customer reviews for further ideas about what makes for comfortable accommodation options in your desired area. Making an informed decision can ensure you are satisfied with all aspects of your holiday experience.

Comparing Amenities

Vacation time is precious, so it's important to consider the amenities offered by your accommodations when selecting a place to stay. Comfort should be a priority when comparing amenities, as should location and cleanliness. Additionally, you should factor in whether you will have access to things like Wi-Fi, a kitchen, or laundry machines. If you are traveling with small children, consider whether the property offers family-friendly services such as cribs, connecting rooms, or organized activities for kids. By thoroughly exploring your options and finding an accommodation that meets most of your needs, you can enhance your vacation experience tenfold.

The Importance of Reading Reviews Before Booking

When researching flights, accommodations, or activities, reviews from other travelers are essential. Not only do they provide an honest, first-hand account of the quality of the product or service being reviewed, but they can also provide additional information that may not be included in the initial research.

When deciding on accommodations, reading reviews can help you determine which places will make for the most enjoyable stay. Reviews offer valuable insight into aspects such as cleanliness and hospitality that can be difficult to assess from online listings or photos. It's also helpful to read up on the cancellation policies of each property and find out what situations may be excluded. Additionally, reading reviews allows you to get an idea of the overall atmosphere of a place before deciding to book it. This can help ensure that your accommodations are well-suited for your needs and expectations.

Here are some tips for reading and understanding reviews:

- **Pay attention to the review date:** Keep in mind that reviews can become outdated over time. If you're reading an old review, it may not be representative of the current state of the product or service. Look for more recent reviews to get a more accurate picture.

- **Consider the reviewer's preferences:** Not everyone

has the same preferences when it comes to travel. Some people may be more sensitive to noise or more particular about cleanliness, while others may be more relaxed. Consider the reviewer's preferences when reading their review to determine if it's relevant to your needs.

- **Look for common themes:** If you're reading multiple reviews, look for common themes. If several reviewers mention the same issue, it's likely that it's a legitimate concern. On the other hand, if the reviews are all over the place, it may be harder to draw any conclusions.

- **Read both positive and negative reviews:** It's natural to focus on positive reviews, but it's essential to read the negative reviews as well. Negative reviews can provide valuable insight into potential problems or issues you may encounter.

You can make more informed decisions about your flights, accommodations, and activities by reading reviews before booking. This can help ensure you have a great vacation and avoid unpleasant surprises.

Checklist of Things to Consider When Choosing Flights and Accommodations

When making travel arrangements for your dream vacation, there are many factors to consider to ensure a smooth and enjoyable experience.

Here is a checklist of things to consider when choosing flights and accommodations:

✓ **Layovers:** Consider the layovers and flight duration when comparing flight options. A longer flight with a shorter layover may be more convenient, but a shorter flight with a longer layover may be more cost-effective.

✓ **Seat preferences:** If you have specific seat preferences, such as a window seat or an aisle seat, consider paying a little extra to ensure you get the seat you want. Also, consider the location of your seat on the plane, as seats toward the front of the plane tend to have more legroom and easier access to the restrooms and overhead bins.

✓ **Flight duration:** Consider the flight duration when comparing flight options. A longer flight may be more cost-effective, but a shorter flight may be more convenient.

✓ **Cancellation policies:** Make sure to read and understand the cancellation policies for your flights and accommodations. This will help you plan for any unexpected changes or emergencies that may arise.

✓ **Additional fees:** Some airlines charge additional fees for things like checked baggage, seat selection, or in-flight meals. Be sure to check for these fees and factor them into your budget when comparing flight options.

✓ **Location of accommodations:** Consider the location of your accommodations when choosing where to stay. If you are looking for a relaxing beach vacation, choose a beachfront hotel. If you are going on a city vacation, you may want to choose accommodations located in the heart of the city and close to attractions.

✓ **Amenities of accommodations:** Consider the amenities important to you when choosing accommodations. Do you want a hotel with a pool and spa or a vacation rental with a fully equipped kitchen?

✓ **Price of accommodations:** Determine your budget and look for accommodations that fit within your budget.

✓ **Distance from attractions:** Consider the distance of your accommodations from the attractions you want to visit. If you want to spend less time traveling, choose accommodations close to the attractions you want to visit.

✓ **Availability of public transportation:** Consider the availability of public transportation when choosing accommodations. If you plan to rely on public transportation during your vacation, choose accommodations that are located near a subway or bus stop.

4. TIPS FOR FINDING THE BEST DEALS

Planning an enjoyable, memorable, and affordable vacation starts with understanding where to look for the best deals. While there is no one-size-fits-all approach to finding great deals, this chapter will provide you with practical tips and insights to help you maximize your budget and make the most of your journey. From researching flights and accommodations to utilizing discounts and other strategies, the right knowledge will ensure you get top value without compromising on quality.

How to Use Comparison Websites Effectively

Taking advantage of comparison websites is an important part of planning any vacation. When utilized correctly, these web tools can help you find the best deals on flights, accommodations, and activities quickly and efficiently. To maximize your savings, start by brushing up on basic search strategies.

The benefits of using comparison websites

Using comparison websites effectively requires you to clearly understand what you are looking for. Of course, it's helpful to know some basic information, such as your destination, date of travel, and the type of service or product you want. It's also important to check what is included in package deals and ensure the cost is right for your budget. Comparison sites provide great value when used this way - allowing you to easily compare different providers on various criteria. As a result, they offer huge benefits by helping you find the best deal possible with minimal effort.

How to compare different options

An effective way to get the most value when using comparison websites is to compare different options. To do so, one should sort the results based on price, filter according to preferences such as flight duration and type of accommodation or use the "flexible dates" feature to test prices for various travel days. By taking these steps, users can make a more informed decision and get the best deal available.

Tips for finding the best deals on comparison websites

The key to finding the best deals when using comparison websites is being flexible with your travel dates and comparing prices across multiple sites. If you plan ahead, you can often book in advance for a better deal, and if you're comfortable leaving the details until the last minute, you can save big. You can also set price alerts so that you know when the price drops or goes up. Remember to read reviews on the website and check their cancellation policies before booking. You can leverage comparison websites to find great deals on your travels with just a few simple steps.

The Benefits of Being Flexible with Travel Dates

One of the most effective ways to save money on your vacation is to be flexible with your travel dates. Here are some reasons why being flexible with travel dates can be beneficial when planning a vacation:

Lower prices

As mentioned above, one of the main benefits of being flexible with your travel dates is that you can often find lower prices on flights and accommodations. Airlines and hotels often have to offer discounted rates to fill seats or rooms that would otherwise go empty, so being open to alternative travel dates can help you take advantage of these discounts.

More availability

By being flexible with your travel dates, you may also have more options for flights and accommodations. If you're set on traveling during peak season, you may find that all the best options are already booked. However, if you're willing to travel during off-peak times, you may have more options to choose from.

Better weather

Depending on your destination, the weather can vary significantly depending on the time of year. By being flexible with your travel dates, you can find better weather conditions at your destination. For example, beach vacations in Hawaii will be significantly cooler and more pleasant during the winter season while sightseeing activities in Northern Europe will be optimal during the summer months. By having the flexibility of choosing different travel dates, you can maximize your vacation experiences and make sure to enjoy ideal weather conditions.

Fewer crowds

In addition to better weather, being flexible with your travel dates can help you avoid crowds. Popular tourist destinations are often busiest during peak season, so if you want to avoid crowds, consider traveling during off-peak times.

Overall, being flexible with your travel dates can provide many benefits, including lower prices, more availability, better weather, and fewer crowds. By considering these factors and being open to alternative travel dates, you can find the perfect vacation at a great price.

Tips for Finding the Best Deals by Being Flexible

One of the most effective ways to save money on your vacation is to be flexible with your travel dates. You can often find significantly lower prices by avoiding peak travel times and searching for flights and accommodations during off-peak periods.

Here are a few tips for finding the best deals by being flexible:

- **Search for flights midweek:** Many people prefer to travel on weekends, so flights on weekdays are often cheaper. Try searching for flights on Tuesdays, Wednesdays, and Thursdays to see if you can find a better deal.

- **Avoid peak travel times:** Peak travel times can vary depending on your destination, but generally, holidays and school breaks are the busiest times for travel. Try to avoid these times to find lower prices on flights and accommodations.

- **Look for last-minute deals:** If you're flexible and able to travel on short notice, you may find discounted rates on flights and accommodations. Keep an eye out for last-minute deals on websites like Expedia or Kayak or consider signing up for alerts from airlines and hotels.

- **Be open to alternative destinations:** If you're flexible with your destination, you may find better deals on flights and accommodations. Consider searching for flights to nearby airports or looking at vacation packages to destinations that are less popular at the time you want to travel.

How to Find Discounts or Coupons

Finding discounts and coupons when planning a vacation can help you save money without sacrificing your desired experiences.

Here are a few places to look for discounts or coupons:

Google

Google is an excellent starting point for locating discounts or coupons - search for combination packages that may be offered as well as regional websites that could provide exclusive deals. Additionally, if you're looking for discounts on specific services like car rental or air travel, use the "site:website.com" search operator to limit your results to that particular website.

Email newsletters

Many airlines, hotels, and travel companies offer discounts or coupons to their email subscribers. If you're planning a trip, consider signing up for newsletters from the companies you're interested in to receive updates on special deals and promotions.

Social media

Many companies offer discounts or coupons to their followers on social media platforms like Facebook, Instagram, and Twitter. Follow your favorite airlines, hotels, and travel companies to stay up to date on their latest promotions.

Loyalty programs

If you're a frequent traveler, consider joining loyalty programs offered by airlines, hotels, and other travel companies. These programs offer members special discounts or rewards, such as free flights or nights, discounted rates, and other perks.

Comparison websites

Websites like Expedia, Kayak, and Orbitz allow you to compare multiple companies' prices for flights, hotels, and vacation packages. By using these websites, you can easily see which options offer the best deals, and you can find discounts or coupons directly through the website.

When using discounts or coupons, it's important to check expiration dates and review the terms and conditions. Be aware of any restrictions or limitations before booking and compare prices with and without the discount to determine if you're getting the best deal.

5. PACKING AND PREPARING FOR YOUR TRIP

Effective packing and preparation are key to a successful trip. This chapter will provide guidelines and strategies for creating a comprehensive packing list and packing efficiently. By following these recommendations, you can ensure you have everything you need for your trip and minimize the risk of forgetting essential items. We will also offer tips for staying organized during the packing and preparation process. By following these best practices, you can minimize stress and ensure a successful and enjoyable trip.

Creating a Packing List

Creating a packing list is an essential step in preparing for a trip. Not only does it help you ensure that you have everything you need, but it also helps you avoid forgetting important items. This is especially important when traveling to a new destination, as you'll need to consider the specific needs and requirements of your trip, such as the weather, activities, and any cultural or practical differences you may encounter. A well-organized packing list can also save you space and weight in your luggage, allowing you to pack only the essentials and avoid unnecessary items. Additionally, it can help you stay within budget by allowing you to plan out exactly what you need and avoid overspending on unnecessary items. Overall, creating a packing list is a crucial step in preparing for a trip and can significantly reduce stress and enhance the overall planning process.

Tips for creating an effective packing list

Creating an effective packing list is essential for any trip, as it helps ensure you have everything you need and helps you avoid forgetting essential items. Here are some tips for creating an effective packing list:

- **Consider your destination, activities, and weather:** Think about where you're going and what you'll do on your trip. Pack clothing and items appropriate for the destination, activities, and weather. For example, if you're going to a beach destination, you'll need swimsuits, sandals, and sunscreen. If you're going on a hiking trip, you'll need comfortable shoes, a hat, and insect repellent.

- **Make a list of essentials:** Start by making a list of essential items you'll need for your trip, such as identification, tickets, medications, and other important documents. Also, pack your charger and any other electronic devices you need, such as your phone, camera, or laptop.

- **Add personal items:** After you've packed your essentials, add personal items such as clothing, toiletries, and any other items you use daily. Consider the length of your trip and the activities you'll be doing when deciding how much to pack.

- **Prioritize what to pack:** If you're limited on space

or weight, prioritize what to pack. Consider which items are most important or necessary, and pack those first. You can always leave room for souvenirs or items you may pick up along the way.

- **Organize your packing list into categories or sections**: Consider organizing your packing list into categories or sections, such as essentials, personal items, and optional items. This can help make it easier to track what you've packed and what you still need to pack.

- **Keep a "running list" of items you need to pack:** As you think of things you need to pack, add them to a "running list" rather than trying to remember everything at once. This can help you avoid forgetting essential items and make the packing process more efficient.

- **Review and update your packing list before you leave:** Before you leave for your trip, review and update your packing list to ensure you have everything you need and remember all important items.

Tips for Packing Efficiently

Are you wondering how to pack everything you need for your trip without overloading your luggage? Packing efficiently is crucial for a smooth and stress-free trip. By using smart packing techniques and packing lighter, you can save space and reduce the burden of lugging around heavy luggage. In this section, we'll provide tips on how to pack efficiently, including strategies for packing lighter, packing hacks to save space, and more.

Here are some tips for packing efficiently and avoiding overpacking:

- **Consider your destination:** Consider the climate and activities you'll be doing at your destination when packing. This will help you determine what clothes and items you'll need, and help you avoid overpacking.

- **Pack multi-purpose items:** Instead of packing multiple items that serve a single purpose, try to pack multi-purpose items that you can use in different ways. For example, pack a sarong that you can wear as a beach cover-up and a scarf instead of bringing both. Other examples of multi-purpose items include a jacket that you can wear as a raincoat or a lightweight layer or a tote bag that you can use as a beach bag or a carry-on for flights.

- **Roll your clothes:** Instead of folding your clothes and placing them in your suitcase, try rolling them up. This will save space and help you fit more clothes into your suitcase.

- **Use packing cubes:** Packing cubes are a great way to organize your suitcase and save space. They allow you to separate your clothes, shoes, and other items into different compartments, which makes it easier to find what you need and prevents everything from becoming a jumbled mess.

- **Use compression bags:** Compression bags are another great space-saving tool. They allow you to compress your clothes and other items, which helps you fit more into your suitcase.

Tips for Packing Lighter

Packing lighter has many benefits, including reducing the burden of carrying heavy luggage and potentially saving money on checked baggage fees. Here are some tips to help you pack lighter and avoid overloading your suitcase:

- **Choose lightweight and multi-purpose items**: Look for lightweight and multi-purpose items to pack, such as a versatile jacket that you can wear in different weather conditions or a scarf that can serve as a wrap or a blanket. Packing items that can be used for multiple purposes can help you reduce the number of items you need to bring.

- **Leave some items behind**: It can be tempting to bring everything you own, but it's important to be selective when packing. Think about what you really need and leave behind any items that you can live without. Consider using travel-size toiletries and skipping items like hairdryers, which are often provided in hotels.

- **Wear your heaviest and bulkiest items:** If you have heavy or bulky items that you need to bring, such as hiking boots or a winter coat, consider wearing them on the plane to save space in your suitcase.

- **Pack smarter with lighter fabrics:** Look for lightweight yet durable fabrics that can help you pack a lighter suitcase. Examples include ultra-lightweight items such as silk, chiffon and cotton blends, and stretchy synthetic materials that don't wrinkle easily. Also, look for things labeled "ultra-light" or "down feather" on the label. These materials can help significantly reduce the weight of your luggage.

- **Limit your toiletries:** Instead of packing full-sized bottles of shampoo, conditioner, and other toiletries, consider using travel-sized bottles or packing solid versions of these products. Consider packing only the essentials and purchasing any additional items at your destination.

- **Pack items appropriate for your destination and activities:** Make sure to pack items that are appropriate for your destination and the activities you'll be participating in. For example, suppose you'll be participating in outdoor activities or traveling to a tropical location. In that case, you may need to bring items like mosquito repellent or sunscreen that are essential for your trip but may add extra weight to your luggage.

By following these tips, you can pack lighter and avoid overloading your suitcase for your trip. Remember also to consider the specific needs and requirements of your destination and activities when packing. Be bold and leave some items behind if they're not absolutely necessary.

Advice on Preparing for Different Types of Vacations

Going on vacation can be an exciting and much-needed break from the daily routine, but it's important to prepare properly for your planned vacation.

Here are some tips for preparing for different types of vacations:

Cruises

- Research the dress code for the cruise line you're sailing with and the destinations you'll be visiting. Some cruise lines have a more formal dress code, while others are more casual. Packing accordingly is important to avoid feeling out of place or underdressed.

- Check the luggage policies for the cruise line. Some cruises have strict size and weight limits for luggage, so check the policies before packing.

- Pack any necessary documents, such as your passport or birth certificate. Some cruises require passengers to have a valid passport, even if you're not leaving the country.

- Consider purchasing travel insurance. Cruises can be expensive, and travel insurance can protect against unexpected events such as trip cancellations or medical emergencies.

- Research the excursions offered by the cruise line. Many cruises offer a variety of excursions at each port of call, ranging from cultural experiences to adventure activities. Consider what you're interested in and book your tours in advance to ensure availability.

Beach Vacations

- Pack plenty of sunscreen, hats, and sunglasses to protect yourself from the sun.

- Bring swimsuits and cover-ups, as well as sandals or flip-flops.

- If you're planning on doing water activities, such as snorkeling or scuba diving, pack any necessary equipment.

- Consider packing lightweight and breathable clothing and layers for cooler evenings.

- Remember beach towels and beach bags to carry all your essentials.

City Breaks

- Pack comfortable walking shoes, as you'll likely be doing a lot of sightseeing on foot.

- Consider packing a lightweight raincoat or umbrella, as cities can often be prone to sudden rain showers.

- Pack a small bag or backpack for carrying essentials such as maps, water, and snacks.

- Consider packing more formal attire if you're visiting a city with a more formal dress code, such as Paris or Rome.

- Research the local customs and culture of the city you're visiting. This can help you avoid making cultural mistakes and ensure a more enjoyable and respectful trip.

Adventure Vacations

- Pack sturdy and comfortable shoes, as you'll likely be doing a lot of hiking or other physical activities.

- Consider packing lightweight and breathable clothing and layers for cooler temperatures.

- If you're planning on doing water activities, such as rafting or kayaking, pack a swimsuit and any necessary equipment.

- Pack any necessary safety equipment, such as helmets and safety harnesses, if you'll be doing activities such as rock climbing or bungee jumping.

- Remember to pack a first aid kit and any necessary medications.

Packing Checklist

To help you make sure you don't forget anything, here is a comprehensive packing checklist:

- ✓ Passport (if traveling internationally)
- ✓ Tickets (flights, tours, etc.)
- ✓ Hotel reservations
- ✓ Cash and credit cards
- ✓ Phone and charger
- ✓ Laptop and charger (if needed)
- ✓ Medications
- ✓ Toiletries (toothbrush, toothpaste, shampoo, soap, etc.)
- ✓ Clothing (shirts, pants, dresses, shoes, etc.)
- ✓ Swimsuit and beach towels (if traveling to a beach destination)
- ✓ Jacket and warm clothing (if traveling to a cold destination)
- ✓ Comfortable walking shoes (if visiting a city)
- ✓ Hiking shoes (if participating in outdoor activities)
- ✓ Sunscreen
- ✓ Hat and sunglasses
- ✓ Camera and charger
- ✓ Snacks and water bottle
- ✓ Travel documents (such as a copy of your passport or travel insurance documents)

Here are a few suggestions for additions to your packing

checklist:

- ✓ Travel adapter or voltage converter (if necessary)
- ✓ Sunglasses case (to keep your sunglasses protected while traveling)
- ✓ Wet wipes (for cleaning your hands or face while on the go)
- ✓ Earplugs (for blocking out noise in hotels or on planes)
- ✓ Travel pillow (for added comfort during long flights or car rides)
- ✓ Insect repellent (if traveling to a destination with mosquitos or other pests)
- ✓ Water purification tablets or a portable water filter (if traveling to a destination with questionable water quality)
- ✓ Travel-sized laundry detergent (for washing clothes on longer trips)
- ✓ Lightweight and compact travel umbrella
- ✓ A small, portable bag or backpack (for carrying essentials while sightseeing or on day trips)
- ✓ A small, portable first aid kit (for minor injuries or emergencies)
- ✓ A small flashlight (for added security and convenience)
- ✓ A lock (for added security when staying in hotels or hostels)
- ✓ Earphones or headphones (for listening to music or watching movies on planes or trains)

Tips for using the checklist effectively

- Review the checklist a few days before your trip to make sure you have everything.

- Consider your destination and activities and add any items specific to your trip to the checklist.

- Consider your travel itinerary and the length of your trip when packing. You'll want to pack enough clothing and other essentials to last the duration of your trip but avoid overpacking by only bringing what you'll actually need.

- Think about the climate and weather at your destination and pack accordingly. This will help you avoid packing unnecessary items or items that may not be suitable for the weather.

- If you're traveling with others, divide the items on the packing checklist among the group to share the load and avoid overpacking.

- Consider the weight and size limits for your luggage, and pack items that are easy to carry and will only take up a little space.

- Make sure to leave some room in your luggage for souvenirs or items you may pick up along the way.

- Keep a copy of the packing checklist with you during your trip in case you need to refer to it or add any items you may have forgotten.

- Feel free to modify the checklist to fit your specific needs. You may find that you need to add or remove items based on your destination and the activities you'll be participating in.

Preparing Your Home for Your Absence

Leaving your home for an extended period can be stressful, especially if you're worried about the safety and security of your home while you're away.

Here are some things you should do to prepare your home for your absence:

- **Lock all doors and windows:** Make sure all doors and windows are securely locked before you leave. This includes any doors or windows that you rarely use, as well as any basement windows or doors leading to crawl spaces.

- **Set your security system:** If you have a security system, ensure it's set and working properly before leaving. If you don't have a security system, consider installing one or setting up a home security camera to keep an eye on your home while you're away.

- **Unplug appliances:** Unplug appliances, such as your coffee maker, toaster, and microwave, to reduce the risk of a fire while you're away. You should also consider unplugging your television, computer, and other electronics to save energy and reduce the risk of a power surge damaging your equipment.

- **Stop mail and newspaper delivery:** If you're going to be gone for an extended period of time, consider stopping mail and newspaper delivery to avoid giving the appearance that you're home. You can also ask a trusted neighbor or friend to pick up your mail and newspapers for you.

- **Arrange for pet care:** If you have pets, make

arrangements for their care while you're away. This could involve hiring a pet sitter or boarding them at a reputable kennel. Ensure your pets have all their necessary documents and medications and leave detailed instructions for their care.

- **Make your home look lived in:** To deter burglars, make your home look lived in while you're away. This could involve using timers to turn on lights, setting your television or radio to turn on and off at random times, or asking a trusted neighbor or friend to park in your driveway or bring your trash cans in and out.

By following the guidelines and strategies outlined in this chapter, you can effectively pack and prepare for your trip. Creating a comprehensive packing list and using smart packing techniques can help you ensure that you have everything you need and avoid forgetting important items.

Staying organized during the packing process can also help reduce stress and enhance the overall planning process. By following these best practices, you can set yourself up for a successful and enjoyable trip.

6. CREATING AN ITINERARY

Planning an itinerary that includes a mix of relaxation and activities is crucial for a successful vacation. In this chapter, we'll give tips on balancing these two elements and provide recommendations for finding the best things to do and see at your destination. By considering your priorities, physical abilities, and the length of your trip, you can create an itinerary that will allow you to enjoy your vacation without feeling overwhelmed or burnt out fully.

Planning an Itinerary that Balances Relaxation and Activities

When planning a vacation, it's important to strike a balance between relaxation and activities. After all, you want to have time to unwind and enjoy your surroundings, but you also want to take advantage of all the things that make a destination unique and exciting. The key is to plan an itinerary that meets your specific needs and interests while leaving room for flexibility and unexpected opportunities. In this section, we'll discuss how to determine your priorities and other important factors to help you create the perfect balance for your vacation.

Determine Your Priorities

Before you start planning your itinerary, take a moment to consider what you want to get out of your vacation. Do you want to relax on the beach or explore the destination? Are you interested in cultural experiences or adventure activities? By determining your priorities, you can create an itinerary that feels meaningful and fulfilling.

To help you determine your preferences, refer back to the section on "Determining the type of vacation that best suits your needs" in Chapter 1 and ask yourself these questions:

- **What are your vacation goals?** Do you want to relax and unwind, have an adventure, or immerse yourself in culture?

- **What are your interests and hobbies?** Consider what activities and attractions you enjoy and look for destinations that offer those experiences.

- **Who are you traveling with?** Are you traveling solo, with a partner, or with a group of friends or family? Your travel companions can greatly impact your vacation goals and priorities.

By answering these questions, you can get a better sense of what you want to get out of your vacation and focus on planning an itinerary that aligns with your priorities.

Plan some downtime

Including some downtime in your vacation plan is essential for maintaining balance and avoiding burnout. No matter how much you love to travel or how action-packed you want your trip to be, it's important to set aside time for rest and relaxation. This can be as simple as lounging on the beach, sitting in a café and people-watching, or taking a leisurely stroll through the destination. Scheduling a massage or spa treatment can also be a great way to relax and rejuvenate. Downtime allows you to unwind and recharge, enhancing your vacation's overall enjoyment. It's also necessary to consider your own physical and mental limits when planning your itinerary. Pushing yourself too hard can lead to burnout and negatively impact the overall enjoyment of your trip. By including some downtime in your vacation plan, you can create a well-rounded and enjoyable trip

Don't overdo it

While it's tempting to pack your itinerary with as many activities as possible when planning a vacation, it's important to remember that you're on vacation to relax. Try not to overdo it and leave some room for flexibility and spontaneity. A jam-packed schedule may seem exciting initially, but it can quickly lead to exhaustion and frustration. To avoid feeling overwhelmed, spread out your activities and allow for some downtime in between. For example, if you're planning a day trip to a nearby town, consider taking a leisurely morning stroll and grabbing a coffee before hitting the road. Or, if you're planning a beach day, give yourself a few hours in the morning to relax and soak up the sun before heading out for a snorkeling excursion. By pacing yourself and allowing for some relaxation, you'll be able to fully enjoy your vacation and avoid feeling burnt out.

Consider your physical abilities

When planning your vacation itinerary, it's important to consider your physical abilities and limitations. If you're planning activities that require a lot of physical exertion, such as hiking, biking, or water sports, make sure you can handle them. It's also important to listen to your body and take breaks as needed to avoid overexerting yourself. This will help you enjoy your vacation to the fullest and avoid any unnecessary injuries or discomfort. If you have any physical limitations or medical conditions, it's a good idea to consult your healthcare provider before planning any strenuous activities. Additionally, consider your age and fitness level when planning your itinerary and choose activities that are suitable for you. By being mindful of your physical abilities, you can have a safe and enjoyable vacation.

Consider the length of your trip

The length of your vacation can significantly impact how you plan your itinerary. If you have a longer trip, you'll have more time to fill with activities and experiences, which can allow for a more leisurely pace and a greater variety of options. However, it's important not to pack too much into your schedule and leave room for flexibility and spontaneous experiences. On the other hand, if you have a shorter trip, you may need to be more selective about what you choose to do and see. In this case, it's important to prioritize your must-see and must-do items and plan your activities accordingly. You may also need to consider the travel time between destinations, as you don't want to spend all your time on the road and not have enough time to enjoy your vacation. By considering the length of your trip and finding a balance between relaxation and activities, you can create an itinerary that allows you to fully enjoy your vacation and avoid feeling overwhelmed or burnt out. Some activities and experiences may be more expensive than others, so it's key to consider your budget when planning your itinerary. You may need to prioritize certain activities over others based on your budget.

Factor in travel time

It's easy to forget to consider travel time when planning a vacation itinerary, especially when you're excited to experience all your destination has to offer. However, it's important to remember that travel time can take up a significant portion of your trip, especially if you're planning a trip with multiple destinations. By factoring in travel time, you can ensure you have enough time to enjoy your vacation and not feel rushed or stressed. Consider the mode of transportation you'll be using and the distance between each destination when estimating travel time. If you are driving, consider the trip's length and any potential traffic delays. If you are flying, factor in the time it will take to get to and from the airport and any layovers or connecting flights. By taking travel time into account when planning your itinerary, you can make the most of your vacation and not feel like you're spending all your time on the road

Leave room for flexibility

Leaving room for flexibility in your vacation itinerary is vital for many reasons. First, it allows you to be open to unexpected opportunities or changes in plans. For example, you might come across a local event or attraction you weren't aware of when planning your trip, and you'll want to have some free time in your schedule to take advantage of it. Additionally, leaving room for flexibility can help you avoid feeling overwhelmed or burnt out. If you pack too much into your itinerary, you might not have enough time to relax and enjoy your vacation. By leaving some free time in your schedule, you can allow for spontaneous experiences and let yourself to take a break and recharge. Finally, flexibility in your itinerary can help you adapt to any changes in your travel plans, such as weather delays or unexpected travel disruptions. By being open to adjusting your itinerary as needed, you can create a more enjoyable and stress-free vacation and help you avoid last-minute stress or disappointment.

Tips for Finding the Best Things to Do and See

Choosing the attractions and activities, you'll experience during your vacation is an exciting and essential aspect of the planning process. There are often many options to choose from, which can be overwhelming. However, with some research and careful consideration, you can find the best things to do and see at your destination that will make the most of your time and budget.

Here are some tips to help you plan an itinerary that will ensure you have a memorable and enjoyable vacation:

Start by doing some research online

One of the most effective ways to find out about the best attractions and activities at your destination is by doing some research online. The internet is a vast resource that can provide you with a wealth of information about your destination. Start by looking for websites and blogs that cover the area you'll be visiting and see what other travelers recommend. You can also use websites like TripAdvisor to read reviews and ratings from other travelers, giving you a sense of what's worth your time and what might not be as enjoyable. By doing some research online, you can get a better idea of the things to do and see at your destination and start planning an itinerary that meets your interests and budget.

Ask locals for recommendations

Asking locals for recommendations can be valuable when planning your vacation itinerary. If you know anyone who has traveled to your destination or if you have local friends or family members, they can provide valuable insights into the best things to do and see. They may be able to recommend hidden gems or local favorites that may not be as well-known to tourists. Locals can also give you an idea of what activities are most suitable for the time of year you'll be visiting, as well as any potential seasonal considerations you should keep in mind. By asking locals for recommendations, you can get a more authentic and personalized experience and make the most of your time at your destination.

Consider off-the-beaten-path experiences

In addition to visiting popular attractions and landmarks, it's also a great idea to consider off-the-beaten-path experiences when planning your vacation itinerary. These can be some of the most memorable and rewarding parts of a trip, as they can give you a more authentic and unique perspective on the destination. To find off-the-beaten-path experiences, consider asking locals for recommendations or do some research online to find hidden gems. These types of experiences can take you away from the crowds and into the heart of the destination, allowing you to fully immerse yourself in the culture and get a feel for the local way of life. By including some off-the-beaten-path experiences in your itinerary, you can have a more well-rounded and fulfilling vacation.

Make a list of your must-see and must-do items

With many options to choose from, it's helpful to prioritize your must-see and must-do list when planning your vacation itinerary. This will help you make the most of your time and budget and take advantage of everything that is meaningful to you. Consider what you're most interested in and what you're willing to sacrifice if you don't have time to do everything. This will help you focus on the experiences and activities that are most meaningful and rewarding to you and allow you to make the most of your vacation. By making a list of your must-see and must-do items, you can ensure that your itinerary is tailored to your interests and preferences, and you'll be able to fully enjoy your trip.

Look for local events and festivals

Attending local events and festivals can be a great way to experience the culture and traditions of a destination. These events can range from cultural festivals and food fairs to music festivals and sporting events. Participating in local events gives you a feel for the local way of life and a more authentic and immersive experience. To find local events and festivals, you can check out local tourism websites or ask locals for recommendations. You might also find information about upcoming events through social media or local newspapers. By looking for local events and festivals, you can add a unique and memorable element to your itinerary.

By following the tips outlined in this chapter, you can create an itinerary that balances relaxation and activities and makes the most of your vacation. Begin by determining your priorities and considering your physical abilities and the length of your trip. Factor in travel time and leave room for flexibility in your itinerary. Then, use online research, recommendations from locals, and off-the-beaten-path experiences to find the best things to do and see at your destination.

Remember to list your must-see and must-do items and look for local events and festivals to add a unique and immersive element to your itinerary. By being mindful of these factors and being open to adjusting your plans as needed, you can create a well-rounded and fulfilling vacation that meets your interests and preferences

7. TIPS FOR ENJOYING YOUR VACATION

Effective vacation planning involves not only choosing the right destination and activities but also considering how to relax and enjoy the experience fully. In this chapter, we will provide practical tips for making the most of your vacation, including strategies for disconnecting from technology, practicing mindfulness, and finding activities that help you relax. We will also offer suggestions for creating lasting memories, such as taking photos, keeping a journal, trying new things, and spending time with loved ones. By following these tips, you can have a fulfilling and enjoyable vacation that leaves you feeling refreshed and rejuvenated.

Relaxing and Unwinding on Vacation

Taking a vacation is an opportunity to relax, unwind, and recharge.

Here are some tips for relaxing and unwinding on your trip:

Disconnect from technology

Taking a break from technology on vacation can be incredibly beneficial for relaxation and enjoyment. While it may be difficult to disconnect completely, there are simple steps you can take to minimize your technology use and fully relax on your trip. Consider setting limits on your screen time and taking regular breaks from screens to unwind and recharge. You can also try setting your phone to "do not disturb" mode to limit notifications or disconnecting from social media and email while you're on vacation. This can help you fully immerse yourself in your surroundings and enjoy your trip without the distractions of technology. Additionally, consider leaving your work email and phone number with a trusted colleague or assistant, so you can truly disconnect and relax on your vacation

Practice mindfulness

Practicing mindfulness on vacation involves bringing your attention to the present moment and letting go of distractions. It is the practice of being present and aware in each moment without judgment. By setting aside time on vacation to practice mindfulness, whether it's through meditation, yoga, or simply taking a leisurely walk and paying attention to your surroundings, you can fully relax and be present in the moment. This can help you fully immerse yourself in your vacation experience and find a sense of calm and relaxation. Additionally, mindfulness practices can help reduce stress and increase feelings of well-being, making for an overall more enjoyable vacation.

Find activities that help you relax

Incorporating relaxation and stress-reducing activities into your itinerary is essential for maintaining balance and avoiding burnout on vacation. While relaxation means different things to different people, some ideas to consider include massages or spa treatments, peaceful walks on the beach, leisurely games of golf, or simply enjoying the sights and sounds of a local café. By setting aside time for these activities and finding what works best for you, you can make the most of your vacation and return home feeling rejuvenated and energized. Whether it's through massage, yoga, or simply taking a moment to appreciate your surroundings, taking time to unwind can enhance your overall enjoyment of the trip.

Suggestions for Creating Lasting Memories

Vacations are a time to create lasting memories with friends and loved ones. Here are some suggestions for creating memories that will last a lifetime:

Take photos

Capturing your vacation through photos can be a great way to remember the experience and relive it in the future. While it's important to take plenty of photos to document your trip, try not to get too caught up in taking pictures and forget to live in the moment.

Consider striking a balance between capturing special moments and enjoying them without the lens of a camera. Remember to take candid shots as well as planned photo shoots and try to capture the feelings and emotions of your trip rather than just the sights. By taking photos and preserving the memories, you can look back on your vacation and relive the experience long after it's over.

Keep a journal

Another way to create lasting memories on your vacation is by keeping a journal. Documenting your thoughts and experiences as they happen can help you capture the unique and special moments of your trip. You can jot down your impressions of new places and experiences or simply reflect on the feelings and emotions that the vacation brings up for you. By keeping a journal, you'll have a record of your trip that you can look back on and cherish for years to come. Whether you prefer a traditional pen and paper journal or a digital version on your phone or computer, make sure to set aside some time each day to write down your experiences and capture the memories of your trip. It's also a great way to relive the memories of your vacation and to share your experiences with others.

Try new things

Taking a vacation is the perfect opportunity to create lasting memories by stepping outside your comfort zone and engaging in some novel experiences. Research has found that engaging in new activities activates the brain's reward system, which helps strengthen the memory of the experience. This means that if you're looking for memorable moments on your next trip, you should try something new.

This could be as simple as sampling a local delicacy or as adventurous as taking part in an outdoor activity. From learning a new language to visiting a place, you've never been before, pushing yourself to do something unfamiliar will create lasting memories and help you grow personally. Don't be afraid to take risks and be open-minded. With a bit of courage, you could find yourself with some of the best memories from your trip!

Spend time with loved ones

Vacations provide an excellent opportunity for strengthening your relationships and creating lasting memories with your family and friends. Plan activities that help you to truly connect with them without the distraction of phones or technology, such as playing board games, going on walks together, cooking meals, or simply enjoying some conversation. Being present in the moment with those who are closest to you can make for some of your most fondly remembered experiences. Make sure to savor every moment and appreciate the quality time spent with them - it will be something that you treasure and look back on fondly in the years ahead.

Set Boundaries

Setting boundaries on vacation is integral for creating lasting memories. When you set boundaries, you have greater control over your time and can create moments that will stick in your memory for years.

Boundaries with yourself are important as they help to define how much time should be spent enjoying activities and taking in the sights versus technology or other distractions. For example, it may be easy to slip into checking your phone every few minutes while out sightseeing or dining with friends—but these moments add up and can detract from the overall vacation experience.

If you are traveling with others, discussing and setting boundaries for tasks like meal preparation, cleaning up, or taking turns choosing activities is important. Establishing clear expectations helps ensure everyone can enjoy the time away together without feeling overburdened with work or responsibility.

Creating lasting memories on vacation requires intentional planning. Keeping a journal and documenting your experiences, trying new activities, forming meaningful connections with loved ones, and setting firm boundaries for yourself are all essential steps to ensure that your journey is filled with unforgettable moments. Although the specifics of each experience may become hazy over time, it's the collective memories of your entire trip that will remain. Therefore, take the time to capture and savor each moment. Engage with your surroundings and make meaningful connections with those around you. These are surefire ways to ensure that when you look back on your vacation, it is a journey that you'll always fondly remember.

8. BONUS: TRAVEL POEMS

Welcome to the bonus chapter of our guidebook! Here, you will find a selection of beautiful travel poems that capture the feeling of wanderlust, adventure, and discovery. All poems in this collection have been copyrighted by the Vacation Countdown App, and if you wish to use any of the poems in this chapter, please be sure to give credit accordingly.

Poetry has a unique ability to capture the beauty and emotion of travel like no other art form. The words evoke feelings of longing, anticipation, joy, and exploration that can transport us around the world. Through these words, we can imagine ourselves in the locations of our dreams or revisit cherished memories from past trips. So, grab a cup of coffee and settle in to explore the world through these inspiring poems. Enjoy!

Exploring the Unknown

Take off your shoes and feel the sand
As it grounds you in a distant land
The sun shines bright, the ocean blue
Awaiting what adventures come anew.

The mountains call from tree-topped peaks
Their secrets lurking beneath Scepters keep
From ancient ruins to bustling cities
There's never a lack of new things to see.

So take your time and wander some more
Let every moment become a chore
Look up at stars in midnight sky
Allowing travel to come alive.

On The Road Again

The open road stretches before me
As far as the eye can see
I pack my bags and hit the road
With nothing but adventure on my mind

I'll go where the wind takes me
To mountains high and valleys low
I'll see the sights and meet new friends
As I journey through the world below

With each new step I take
I'll embrace all that comes my way
For every twist and every turn
Brings a new and wondrous day

So come and join me on my journey
And see all that the world has to offer
For life is too short to stay put
So, let's explore and discover!

Journeying to Unknown Worlds

Look to the sky and soar over distant horizons
Seeking new adventures and a world of wonders and
delight
Ride the waves of sea's embrace
As you wander an unknown place.

Explore nature's gifts with endless grace
Treasure each moment, don't forget to trace
The memories and stories they will tell
Of a journey to discover the secrets of distant lands so
well.

Discover the mysteries of foreign cultures
Unlock the wonders of faraway places
Find new paths and new heights above
As you explore with curiosity and love.

Memories on Board

A cruise to remember, that's what they say
But I soon learned the truth while I was away.

The rocking boat and long wait for food
The early morning drills not always in a good mood.

The ports of call with crowded streets
Where you spend all night trying to find seats.

Excursions that are far too expensive
Long lines where you'd grow quite defensive.

But still, we made the best of each day!
Exploring all around, come what may!

On shore excursions we'd take our time
Seeing beautiful sights that made us feel so sublime.

And at night we'd gather on the deck
Where memories were made lasting until we had to deck!

Yes, a cruise to remember for sure
A fantastic journey from which there's no cure!

Adventure Awaits

I love to travel and explore
The world is my oyster, that's for sure
I'll go wherever the wind takes me
From mountaintops to the deep blue sea

I'll wander through ancient cities
And marvel at the pyramids so grand
I'll hike through rainforests
And bask on sandy beaches with a tan

I'll try new foods and learn new phrases
As I immerse myself in different cultures and ways
I'll meet new friends and make new memories
On this journey through the world, it's true

So come and join me on my adventures
We'll see all that the world has to share
For life is too short to stay put
Let's explore and discover what's out there!

Exploring alone

Gone is the pressure of what to do or say,
For I'm on a mission to explore my own way.
I'll venture off into unknown territories,
And make decisions based on what I truly desire.

No more worries of expectations and standards,
For I'm here to find my own answers.
The memories made will be unlike any other,
For the only comparison is the one within myself.

My spirit will soar through new lands,
As I jump into exciting unknown plans.
I'll discover what it means to truly live and love,
As I shed the expectations of what it should be like.

With each journey, I'll find more than a destination,
For this solo vacation brings inner transformation.
The beauty in being alone can't be measured or contained,
For a lifetime of joy is found when we let go of our chains.

A Road Trip to Remember

The family trip was meant to be fun
But what we never saw were the hidden surprises that
would come.
From bickering kids in the back seat
To arguments over where each night we'd sleep.

We got lost on our way, taking turns for guidance
Mom and Dad grumbling under their breath in silence.
On the road, we had to stop for food
But of course, no one agreed on what sounded good.

We made our way through forests and mountains so high
But then it started to rain and everyone wanted to cry.
The kids were getting cranky, someone was always bored
And, of course, we forgot the all-important snacks at
home.

But despite all the bumps along our way
We still managed to laugh and make memories that will
stay.

So don't forget when you plan your vacation getaway

That it's not always sunshine and joy, but lots of laughs

along the way!

Living the Beach Life

The sun is shining, a perfect day,
We set up our towels, put on our hats.
I feel my toes in the warm sand,
We walk down the shore hand in hand.

We take a break to have a snack of fruit,
Watching birds soar above us.
The beach is our playground, we laugh and play,
Living life under the sun's golden rays.

We collect some seashells on the way back,
This is the life we've been waiting for!
No matter how far I go or where I roam,
I carry this beach life with me wherever I go.

The sand between my toes, the sun on my face,
A reminder that some things cannot be replaced.
So when you're feeling lost and your spirit is low,
Remember the beach life that we all enjoy!

ABOUT THE PUBLISHER

Kulana Media Productions LLC is a digital media company with more than two decades of experience in creating web and mobile solutions. Our expansive portfolio includes 500 websites and 100 applications, including the highly sought-after Vacation Countdown App. The app has been featured in various news outlets and it has been downloaded millions of times by passionate users all around the globe.

We want to take this opportunity to thank our users for their trust and feedback. Numerous reviews, comments, and emails have allowed us to improve our Vacation Countdown App and provide the best experience for our users.

Our first book, this Guidebook for Planning the Perfect Vacation is an exciting milestone for our company. By combining decades of digital media expertise with our passion for travel, we have created a one-of-a-kind resource to help you get the most out of your vacation planning. Our mission is to help people plan the perfect vacation without any hassle or stress, making sure that their dream getaway turns out even better than they have imagined.

Thank you for trusting us with your precious time and we hope you have enjoyed our book and look forward to more in the near future. Please do not hesitate to contact us at info@vacationcountdownapp.com if you have any questions or feedback. This would not just help us create more interesting books, but also provide valuable insight into what our readers are looking for. We would love to hear from you so that we are able to better cater to your needs as well as expectations.

Printed in Great Britain
by Amazon